BY THE POWER
OF GOD
LIVING THE TRUE CHRISTIAN LIFE

Vincent Vetere

**Arm Wrestler, Corrections Officer,
Magician, Break-Dancer,
and Evangelist**

WESTBOW
P R E S S®
A DIVISION OF THOMAS NELSON
& ZONDERVAN

Scripture taken from the King James Version of the Bible.

WestBow Press books may be ordered through
booksellers or by contacting:

WestBow Press
A Division of Thomas Nelson & Zondervan
1663 Liberty Drive
Bloomington, IN 47403
www.westbowpress.com
1 (866) 928-1240

ISBN: 978-1-4908-9068-5 (sc)
ISBN: 978-1-4908-9529-1 (e)

Print information available on the last page.

WestBow Press rev. date: 09/21/2015

For my dad and mom, Frank and Anna Vetere, who have been, from the beginning, the two best parents a son could have. They are, and have always been, there to support me, no matter what.

For my beautiful bride, Andrea, who is beautiful on the inside as well as on the outside.

For my in-laws: Andy, who led me to the Lord in 1986, and Edie, who always had a soft-spoken word of encouragement.

And for my two beautiful children, Vanessa and Danielle. They bring me so much joy, and I am very blessed and privileged to watch them grow into the mature young women they are becoming.

Whatever you do, work at it with all your heart,
as working for the Lord, not for human masters.
Colossians 3:23

PREFACE

It all started when I was about fourteen years old, and I became a break dancer. By the time I was sixteen, my troupe performed for Donald Trump at Trump Towers. We were the opening act for Tina Turner, and we performed for John Lennon's son at the Waldorf Astoria. Finally, we gave a big break-dancing performance at Madison Square Garden in 1984 for the Harvest Moon Ball.

In 1986 I committed my life to living for God completely. I took every Bible class offered at my church, Bethlehem Assembly of God in Valley Stream, New York. I then went to Christ for the Nations Bible School.

In 1990 I became a New York City corrections officer and worked at Rikers Island. They held their police Olympics every year, and I entered it and won in the armwrestling. I won the New York State Police gold medal four years in a row. Then I flew to Washington, DC, for the International Law Enforcement Games in arm wrestling and won the gold medal again. I also won the Empire State Golden Arms tournament at the USS Intrepid in arm wrestling and received the MVP award.

In 1997 I became a magician/illusionist, and from then until now, I have done over four thousand shows some with over four thousand people in attend anceand have ministered all over the United States and abroad.

In 2014 *Good Morning America* and the United Kingdom press interviewed me about law enforcement and arm wrestling, and *Good Morning America* included a segment about my being a magician.

I have written this book so that you may know the power of God in every area of your life. If you allow the Lord to have complete control of your life, and you stay humble before Him, He will lift you up. If you allow pride to set in, get ready to fall.

CHAPTER 1

The Beginning

"And whatsoever ye do, do it heartily, as to the Lord, and not unto men; knowing that of the Lord ye shall receive the reward of the inheritance: for ye serve the Lord Christ" (Colossians 3:23 KJV).

When I was a young kid of about fourteen years old, I started to learn how to break-dance. Break dancing was the coolest form of dance at that time, and my friends came over every day to practice. We learned how to spin on our backs and on our heads, do windmills, and do flips off another person's back. We had so much fun!

Then one day we went to a dance at Roller Castle, a roller skating place. When we did our break dancing there, the place went wild. A couple of agents happened to be there looking for new talent, and when they saw us, they immediately took us in. They started booking us for break-dancing shows and battles all over the New York area, and we were called the New York City Spin Masters.

Throughout the years, we performed all over the tristate area and in almost every club, restaurant, and catering hall in New York City not to mention being driven around in limos. We were the opening act for Tina Turner at Trump Towers, and we did a show for John Lennon's son at the Waldorf Astoria in New York City. We performed at Madison Square Garden for the 1984 Harvest Moon Ball, which attracted some of the best break-dancers of that time.

Talk about living an amazing life! We were, as some might say, walking on water! We had hit the top, and there wasn't any higher place to go.

So, what happened?

CHAPTER 2

The Answer

Like most things in life, break dancing faded out, and we weren't on top of the world anymore. I had always known that drugs and alcohol weren't the answer to my problems because my parents had taught me right from wrong. But there was a big emptiness inside me, and for a while, I just went through the motions of living day-by-day, searching for the meaning of life and why I was here.

I do remember crying out to God one day and saying that there had to be more to life than just waking up, going to school, watching TV, riding my bike, or going to the mall or the beach. All of these things were good to do, but they weren't giving me the awesome feeling I'd gotten from the break dancing.

I had a beautiful girlfriend. I had excellent parents who loved me very much and were always there for me, no matter what. I had a cool sister. I had good friends, who, even though they sometimes let me down, were cool too, for the most part.

So, why was I still so empty on the inside?

CHAPTER 3

My Girlfriend's Dad

My girlfriend Andrea went to a Christian church called Bethlehem Assembly of God in Valley Stream, New York. She called her father Andy, and he was this really cool guy who was into martial arts, boxing, and knife throwing. He had a really cool gym in his garage, and he taught me how to hit the speed bag and punching bag, and how to move my head and body so I wouldn't get hit back in a real fight. It was cool just to hang around his garage gym.

Andy also had all these words written on the walls, and at the time, and I had no idea what they were. They said things like: "Except a man be born again, he cannot see the kingdom of God" John 3:3 and "Whosoever will call upon the name of the Lord shall be saved." Romans 10:13 He also had stuff written on his heavy bag. I had no idea what it all meant, but there was one thing that really stood out on the wall. It said, "He that loves mother or father more than me is not worthy of me, and if somebody loves son or daughter more than me, he is not worthy of me." Matthew 10:37

Andy saw me looking at the words, and he started to explain the meaning of it all. When he mentioned that they were all in the Bible, I was completely lost because I really didn't know what the Bible was. All I knew was that it was some religious book.

Then Andy explained that the Bible was God's Word. He was really focused on it. He said that if I really understood what "God's Word" meant, I would want to know everything there was to know about it. He said that the Bible was the best-selling book in the world, that it was illegal in many countries, and that it contained the meaning of life. He even quoted a verse that said, "My people are destroyed for lack of knowledge."

He said that if I wanted to know the meaning of life, the reason I'd been created, and my purpose in being alive, it was all in the Bible. The main reason that so many people are so lost and empty is because they are looking for anything to fill the void in their lives. What they are really missing is a true personal relationship with Jesus.

Then he explained a little more of who Jesus was and some of the amazing things He'd done like walking on water, healing sick people, and raising people from the dead. Andy also mentioned how tough Jesus was, because He knew that He was going to take a beating and be tortured and killed for me. Jesus had the power to stop the torment at any time, but He loved me so much that he endured the cross for me.

Andy said that anybody can do wrong, and most people do, but that it takes a real man to stand up for what is right and then do it. He said that God wanted 100 percent of my heart, that He wanted me to live for Him in every area of my life.

Something else caught my attention. He said that a little kid had more guts than me if she was lifting up the name of Jesus. I said, "Okay, count me in." And right there in the garage, I asked Jesus into my life. I asked Him to help me be the man I was born to be. Andy said that this was the most important decision in my life and that I could now know for sure that I would have eternal life up in heaven.

CHAPTER 4

The Study

From the day I gave my heart to God, I took every Bible class that my church had to offer. I was there three or four times a week, trying to soak in as much of the Bible as I could. The youth leader was Steven Milazzo, who had a fire for the Lord and was hungry to see people live the Christian life to the fullest. He was always encouraging me to trust God, pray every day, and study the Scriptures. He didn't just preach it; he lived it. That was in 1986, and now he is the lead pastor of Bethlehem Assembly of God in Valley Stream, New York.

Later, I went to a Bible college called Christ for the Nations in Stonybrook, New York. That school had some of the best teachers. Dennis Bambino was a teacher who usually spoke in fire-and-brimstone messages. He talked about being dead to your own plans and alive to God's plans. All I wanted to do was soak up his class.

Then there was Gary Zarlengo, who was very good at teaching practical ways of living the fullest Christian life. He used visual aids to helps us remember biblical truths.

I was there to learn everything that God had planned for me. I took classes on evangelism, Old and New Testament survey, Christ the healer, doctrinal foundations, children's ministries, and many more. These classes helped to clarify my purpose in life. The closer I got to God, the more I understood that people would always let me down for one reason or another, but that God would never let me down and I needed to trust Him in everything. I was still very young and had a trusting spirit.

When you read this book, you can see why choosing to live for Christ is, by far, the best decision a person can ever make. All the answers for dealing with life, people, and trials are in the Scriptures. It's our job to search for those answers.

CHAPTER 5

New York City Corrections

In 1990 I became a New York City corrections officer and worked at Rikers Island, which is the largest prison complex in the United States. We had to deal with inmates who were the worst of the worst. The jails were out of control, and it was our job to gain it back. The use of force between inmates and officers was growing fast, and violence was everywhere.

One day I was on duty during the inmate lunch, and there were between five and six hundred inmates there. I heard a lot of noise down the corridor, so I ran toward it. There I saw several inmates and officers fighting, and blood was everywhere. I pulled the first inmate off my partner, and then I heard somebody yell, "Vetere, watch out!"

As soon as I ducked down and turned around, an inmate punched me across my jaw and then wrapped his arm around my neck. By then, my heart was pounding fast, and I immediately grabbed his wrist with one hand and his elbow with the other in an attempt to throw him, judo style. Unfortunately, he had braced himself, and in doing so, his elbow snapped across my shoulder. Then we both fell to the ground.

I still didn't let go, because not only was he screaming, but he was still trying to hit me. As we were on the ground fighting, his wrist spun completely around, and that was the end of that fight.

When it was all said and done, my jaw was swollen, and he had a cast the length of his whole arm. Then he was put in the "bing," which is a twenty-three-hour lock-in, for thirty days. My partner had gotten about ninety stiches across his head after getting hit with a solid steel object.

From the time I first got on the job, we were in some kind of use-of-force situation almost every day. Officers and inmates were going to the hospital all the time with bumps, bruises, and stab or slash wounds. It continued to be like this until we got the jails under control.

Red Alert: Possible Escape

It was a beautiful and quiet day outside of Rikers Island. We had just finished working our tour of duty and were ready to go home, when suddenly we heard an alarm go off and the announcement, "Red alert, inmate missing. Possible escape!"

In that situation, Rikers Island instantly shuts down. Nobody leaves, and all inmates go back to their housing areas. Emergency services search the area with dogs. Extra harbor boats check the waters, and spotlights are set up all over the place. The officers all come together to form a perimeter around the entire island, so there is no way somebody will get past us without our knowing. The stress level is rocket-high, but the walls are closing in on the missing inmate.

On this occasion, the dogs confirmed that an inmate was missing from the jail but that he was still hiding on Rikers Island. That was a little comforting, but where was he? After about five days, we found him between the walls and the fence game over.

CHAPTER 6

Short Story about Forgiveness

I had a supervisor I worked with for several years. I always looked out for him and took care of minor problems so he didn't have to, and he always thanked me for it.

Then one day, a problem occurred, and he left me totally stranded, completely betrayed and I was going to get written up for it. He was scared to even look at me because he knew he was in the wrong, and I was taking the blame for him. But he also knew that one of us was going to get written up, so he looked out for himself and left me.

I understand about forgiveness for the most part, so I chose to forgive him completely, from my heart. I felt freed in making that choice, but the storm was still to come.

The supervisor two ranks higher than my supervisor came to me and said, "Vetere, I know you're a stand-up man and God-fearing, so I'm gonna let you go. I don't need a report or any paperwork. I said, "Thank you, sir," and that was it.

My entire career was very much like that. As you can see, it always pays to live the Christian life, no matter where you live or work.

CHAPTER 7

Prayers Answered

On Rikers Island, there are positions outside the jail in security, transportation, the harbor unit, groundskeeping, and so on. To transfer into those jobs, you usually have to know somebody, or you have to have spent a lot of time on your current job.

I knew a big boss and gave him my paperwork, requesting a change. He got back to me in a few days and said he couldn't help me, because I didn't have enough time on the job. The job I wanted was usually for people who were ready to retire. I said, "Thanks anyway," and then I took my transfer paperwork and submitted it to the personnel department. I asked God if He would help me with this transfer. I wanted to work in Rikers Island security or the harbor unit, so I sent applications to both, but I really didn't believe it was going to happen.

Then one day I got called in to personnel. I was a little scared because the only time they call you is if something is wrong. When I got there, the captain said, "Congratulations. Your transfer was approved. You start Monday."

I was in shock, but I guess I shouldn't have been, because I'd had the *real* big boss on the job: God. It also happened that the two positions I'd wanted in the harbor unit or security had been separate at the time I applied, but when they made the new positions, they merged the two. So I got both security *and* harbor unit double blessings!

After a while, I got called to the corrections academy to help teach the new recruits some self-defense for use in dangerous situations. While working as a corrections officer, I had been trained in many things: weapons, communication, law, people skills, first aid, forensic science, and so on.

Working as an officer had been an adventure in itself. I'd had to work on Christmas, New Year's, Fourth of July, and my kids' birthdays, and I'd missed family weddings. It was all part of the job, and if I wanted to finish my career, I had no other choice. My wonderful wife understood it all and always supported me. I thank God for my beautiful bride, Andrea!

CHAPTER 8

Let's Talk About Arm Wrestling

Back in 1991, my supervisor told me about possibly representing New York City corrections at the New York State Police Olympic Games in arm wrestling. I said, "Sure," because I had just been learning how to arm-wrestle from my friend Jason Vale. He was one of the best arm wrestlers in his weight class, and he had won many competitions. One of the first things Jason said was to keep God first in arm wrestling. Then he started to teach me how to train for the event. Here are some of the secrets he came up with:

- Make sure you're in good health, and study more about health and exercise before you start any training.
- Pray before practice and competition.
- Remember that it doesn't matter if you win or lose. What matters is how you handle the situation. Always give God the glory.

- Train to win the prize (1 Corinthians 9:24). Read the Scriptures and put them into practice.

Arm Wrestling Techniques

Technique #1: The Hook

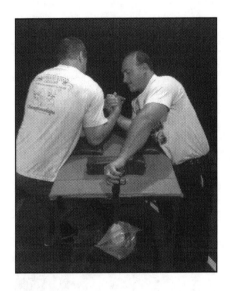

Warm up for about fifteen minutes in the "hook" position. This is where you curl your wrist in a hooked position against your opponent's arm and wrist and pull toward yourself and to the side. Jason and I did this back and forth to get some good blood flowing into our arms. Always remember to keep your body as close to your arm as possible. Keep breathing and stay focused.

The "hook" is what most amateurs do, but it is a very good strategy if you are stronger than the other person. You will most likely win with it because arm wrestling is mostly about strength. But if you go against somebody who knows a move called the "top roll" you will probably lose. What the top roll does is to take away most of the power of the hook position, which then gives the other guy the win.

Technique #2: The Top Roll (with Robert Grover)

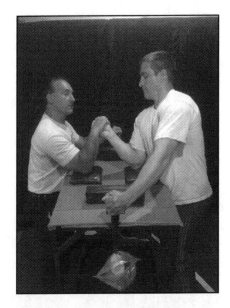

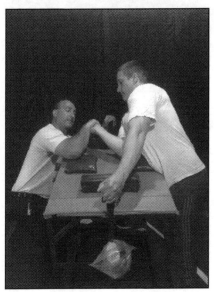

This is a more advanced move among professional arm wrestlers, and this is how it works. When you lock up hands, you focus on pulling your arm back toward yourself, trying to make your opponent's arm open up. Keep pulling your back knuckles toward your face, as this will take the power away from someone doing the hook. It will make his wrist go backward and his arm should extend. This will, in turn, make it easier to pull him down to the side.

If you normally work out with weights, the top roll is like doing a hammer curl. You keep the dumbbell in a horizontal position and go up and down several times. Then, stop at the top position, bend your body forward, and continue holding the weight. This will help you get stronger in back pressure, which is key for this move.

While trying to do the top roll, you can also try to slide your fingers up and over the top of your opponent's hand, which will give you even more leverage. It's not always easy, but if you practice, you will get the feel of how to creep your fingers up over a person's hand.

Technique #3: The Shoulder Press

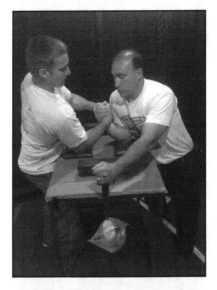

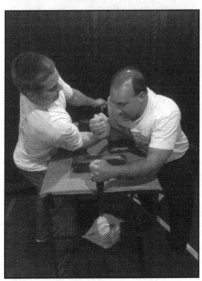

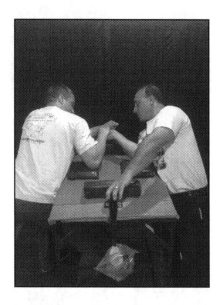

Here is another power type of move. This is where you bring your shoulder as close to your opponent's arm as possible, without your arm touching your shoulder. Then use your triceps and shoulder to push down on your opponent's arm, all the way to the pad. Sometimes your wrist will flop backward, but that doesn't matter. If you get his arm down, it will still be a win.

Exercises Specific to Arm Wrestling

1. Wrist Curls (Rob Grover)

This is where you grab a dumbbell or a straight bar with your wrist facing up and add weights. Sit down on a bench, and let your arms hang off your knees or the bench. Use just your wrist to lower and lift up the weight. After several repetitions, you should hold the weight up as long as you can. Keep working in this area, as it is excellent training for forearm strength.

2. Bicep Curls (Tommy Wierman)

This is where you grasp the weight with your palms up, using a dumbbell or straight bar, and curl your arm up from a down position all the way up, close to your shoulder and then lower it again. This also keeps the weight up, just as it does in wrist curls. This is good for pulling the other guy's arm away from his body.

3. Hammer Curls

This is almost exactly the same as the biceps curl, except that you hold the weights with your palm in a vertical position as you raise your arm up and down.

4. Reverse Wrist Curls

This is similar to the wrist curl, except that you hold the weights with your palms facing down and use only your wrist to go up and down. This will mostly work the arm to use the top roll.

5. Hand Grippers or Hand Ball

This is an excellent exercise to help develop finger pressure, which causes your opponent to have to deal with your hand as well as your arm—another tool in your arsenal. As in all exercises, remember to hold the position as long as possible, so when you squeeze the ball or hand gripper, remember to hold it closed as long as you can.

6. Bungee Cord around Pole

This is my favorite exercise. The bungee cord is an elastic cord that you can get at most sports stores. I wrap it around a solid pole, pull it in an arm wrestling position, and try to hold it as long as I can. This helps to give you endurance and strength. As you pull, turn your body in various positions. This will mimic all different people's arms, so you will be ready for anybody.

7. Practice Bouts

Try to arm-wrestle many people bigger and stronger people, if possible. That will help you deal with all types of arms and pressure. It is to your advantage to keep training until you feel a good burn.

8. Protein

Eating enough protein is very important because it fuels your muscles and helps you get stronger.

9. Staying Squared-Off

It is important to always keep your arms squared off with your body during a match, as there is a position we call a "break arm position." Let's say that you're arm-wrestling right-handed and you turn your body too much to the left. If the other guy is pulling your arm to the right, you can really get hurt, so don't do it. Besides, there isn't any power there anyway. Keep your body squared with your arm, and use all the moves I've described.

The Day of the Competition

I had done all I could to train, and I was off to upstate New York to compete in the New York State Police Olympic Games in arm wrestling.

The grand ballroom could hold over a thousand people, and from the look of things, there were over a thousand people who had showed up to arm-wrestle or to spectate. The pressure was on. We all got weighed in and put into our weight classes. I was in the 175-pound class, and it was stacked with competitors from all over New York state.

When they called my name to come to the table, nobody knew who I was. I was just some officer from corrections. When they called my opponent's name, I saw that he looked like a super body builder with biceps that looked like they had baseballs on them.

From the look of things, there was no way I should even be in this guy's class. When we locked up arms, I looked even smaller, and he looked like he was going to break my arm in half.

The ref said to him, "Are you ready?" Then he asked me, "Are you ready?" Then the ref said, "Go!"

I pulled so fast and hard that his arm went down, and I'd won in less than a second! The crowd went wild, standing to their feet in disbelief and amazement, shocked at what they had just seen. Match after match, each one was just like the first, and by now everybody was chanting my name: "Vinny, Vinny, Vinny." After I'd won my weight class, I taught the spectators and other arm wrestlers some technique, and I had my picture taken with them.

After winning the gold medal four years in a row, I was asked to represent New York in the International Police Olympic Games held in Washington, DC. To make a long story short, it turned out the same as the New York State Police Olympics: I won every match in less than a second.

And during the interview that followed, I shared about arm wrestling and my faith in God.

Jason Vale

CHAPTER 9

The Interview

Every year, the news broadcasters interviewed me, asking how it felt to be the reigning champ and defending champ, asking how I trained, and so on. I always told them what we do and how hard we train, describing all the hours of blood and sweat and all the secrets. I said that winning was a great feeling and that the excitement in the air helped to give me energy.

I also told them that the most important thing about arm wrestling was that, whether I won or lost, God was going to get the glory. For some reason, they always cut out the part about God when it went on TV except for last year, because the interview was live, and everybody was in the camera area, so the whole interview was automatically broadcast on the news, ha-ha! This happened on a segment called "New York Arm Wrestling Association, Empire State, New York golden arms tournament of champions," which was hosted by Gene Camp (nycarms.com) and was the biggest venue there was. I was on fire in arm wrestling and on fire for the Lord.

The American Arm-Wrestling Association was hosting a championship on the *USS Intrepid*, the air/sea ship, in New York City. Everybody was going to be there for this one. It was open to all the winners of previous competitions throughout the area.

The entire *Intrepid* was packed with arm wrestlers and spectators all over the ship. The ship was docked in New York City waters and overlooked the beautiful Manhattan skyline. It was a beautiful day. Old-timers and newcomers alike were there, getting ready to compete for the "most valuable player" award.

After weigh-in was done, the games began. I was in the 175- to 200-pound weight class. I could have stayed in the lower class, but my friend was there, and I was heavier than he was, so I went up in weight. When my matches began, all of them were over super fast, just as they'd been in the police Olympics. In less than .01 second, the match was over unless I knew that the other guy was new and was not really good. Then I would go slowly to make it look good for his friends and family before I won.

With my last match, I won the 175- to 200-pound class. Then, for some reason, I fell asleep in some corner on the ship. Suddenly, I heard people calling my name: "Vinny, Vinny!" I woke up, and they said I had to challenge for the most valuable player award. I must have forgotten about that, ha-ha!

Most Valuable Player

In this particular event, the lightweight winners went up against each other, and then the heavyweights competed. The winners of both categories would then compete in the final match.

Okay, here is the recap of events. We were on the *USS Intrepid* for the biggest arm wrestling competition held by the New York Arm-Wrestling Association, and we had just completed hours upon hours of matches in categories for men, women, masters, and lefties. There were two final contestants competing for the most valuable player award. One was the undefeated, three-hundred-pound guy who had won the superheavy weight class. The other was me, floating around 175 pounds and undefeated in my weight class. As a matter of fact, the other guy's last match hadn't even happened, because his opponent, who had just won his own heavyweight class, said there wasn't any way he could beat this guy. So now it was him against little ol' me.

The MVP Match

"Eye of the Tiger," the music theme from the movie *Rocky*, was playing. My opponent and I came up for pictures, and we looked like David and Goliath. Then he went to his side of the table, put chalk on his hands, and started shaking the table and screaming. He had this look in his eyes like he was going to kill me, just like when Rocky was fighting Thunderlips in Rocky 3.

I put chalk on and came to table.

Now the crowd was screaming and standing to their feet. As soon as we locked our hands, it went completely silent. You could hear a pin drop. It was so crazy!

We were both trying to get a good grip, but it got to the point where the ref had to adjust our hands. We weren't allowed to move, or it would have been a foul. Chalk was falling from our hands. The ref looked at him and asked, "Are you ready?" He said yes. Then the ref looked at me and asked, "Are you ready?" I said yes. Then he said, "Ready, go!"

I hit him so fast and hard and with so much force that the table shook. Chalk went flying, and his arm hit the pad with a loud thump. The crowd went ballistic. I had just won the most valuable player award from among the best arm wrestlers at the New York Empire State Golden Arms competition. Wow!

When it came time to award the trophies and take pictures, the crowd started chanting, "Speech! Speech!" So they gave me the mic. The first thing I said was, "I can do all things through Christ who strengthens me." I said it didn't matter if I won or not. What mattered was that God got the glory.

The crowd was cheering, "We love you, Vinny," and I said it back to them. I wanted to represent this sport in a good way by being the people's champion and always giving God the glory. Then I went out to the crowd and started helping kids and their parents learn the sport. They wanted to take pictures with me, just like they had during the police Olympics. It was really cool.

CHAPTER 10

The Magic, Arm Wrestling, and the Hiatus

Okay, here's another recap.

I won the gold medal for four years in the New York Police Olympics. Then I flew down to Washington, DC, for the International Police Olympics and won their gold medal too. After that, I entered the Empire State Arm Wrestling Tournament and won that too as well as the most valuable player award. So I planned to retire from the sport for the time being.

I'd gotten married to a beautiful girl named Andrea, who gave me two beautiful daughters, Vanessa and Danielle.

Rikers Island prison was on a high alert, and we were working mandatory seventeen-hour days. When I was off, I chose to spend all my time with my family and kids. God was steering me in new direction.

I was also building my magic show business, which grew really fast. Before long, I was doing illusions and magic all across the tristate area New York, New Jersey, and Connecticut. My audiences ranged from little kids' parties to black-tie affairs for the CEOs of major business corporations. Public schools, synagogues, and Christian assemblies were booking me months in advance.

I started to add a lot more messages to the show. For instance, I would have somebody strap me in a strait jacket, and then I would escape. The accompanying message was about how to escape the bondage we face every day. Sometimes I wore a black mask and made it float in the air, change color, and then multiply. The message was about self-image: about not hiding behind a mask, learning to be yourself, remembering that God doesn't make any junk, and knowing for sure who you are in God.

I started doing gospel magic messages all over the place for men's ministries, youth groups, marriage ministries, vacation Bible schools, youth conventions, Teen Challenge, and drug rehab. I never compromised my message, and I had strong views about sin and the results of it. I presented a show that was tailored to the age group and the occasion, and I was usually booked several months in advanced. The show was usually fun and exciting, and we engaged as many people as possible.

Here's one example of a show I did at a marriage seminar, where I had a husband and wife come up on stage. I borrowed the woman's wedding ring, made it disappear, made a few jokes about it, and got everybody laughing. Then I had the husband walk all the way to the other side of the stage by himself and open up several colorful boxes only to find his wife's wedding ring in the last box. At that point, there was always thunderous applause.

I had the husband get on one knee, put the ring back on his wife's finger, say "I love you," and give her a hug and kiss. After that, I gave a short message, saying, "What God has joined together, let no man or magician separate." I have gotten many positive testimonies from people who attended the marriage gospel message shows.

Some of my favorite shows are where there is a big tent set up outdoors in a park or field. People gather all around, filling the seats, and then we start the show. It's such a blessing to watch people enjoy the show while hearing the message about the Lord. Afterward, I have our prayer team meet with people to answer any questions.

My family is also a part of the show. It's great having them along when we are able to go on mission trips and do the gospel show for thousands at a time. My sixteen-year-old was able to get up in front of four thousand people and share what it's like growing up in a Christian family. My thirteen-year-old loves to perform, is excellent at ad lib, and is comfortable in front of large groups.

I remember doing shows where I made the CEO (or pastor or guest of honor) appear from an empty box. Then I laid the person down on a flat table, covered him, and floated him all over the stage. By then, the audience was clapping loudly. Then I pulled the cloth away to show that he had vanished, only to reappear at the back of the audience with pink slips for the employees. The audience always got to their feet for a standing ovation.

My family has always been part of the shows in some way or another. We do around 200 to 250 shows a year, in case you were wondering.

Even for kids' shows, we had really cool messages. We made money come out of their ears, arms, hands, noses, and so on, until they were screaming, "Check my ears!" Of course, they always had some whenever

I checked. Then I gave the message in a way they could understand. I told them that the love of money was the root of all evil not that money was evil but that the *love* of it was.

I don't advertise, but the number of referrals I get is off the charts. Most of the time, people book us on the same day they see the show or within a week afterward. When I'm performing for public functions and schools, I know the limits of what I can say and what I can't.

CHAPTER 11

The Return to Arm Wrestling

Back in 2002, my beautiful bride, Andrea, said that there was an arm wrestling competition in Rockville Centre, which was five minutes from my house. I said I would compete, but I was really scared because my whole family was going to be there aunts, uncles, cousins, and so on and I hadn't arm-wrestled in about six years.

When I got there, everybody remembered me and wondered where I'd been. I told them, but then I tried to stay focused on the competition. This was my first time in an old-fashioned sit-down tournament, but that didn't seem to matter, because I won all my matches very fast. When it was over, I'd won my weight class.

Then came the announcement that there would be an overall champ, which meant that I was going to have to go against my friend and mentor in arm-wrestling, Jason Vale, who had won the heavyweight class.

Before I knew how to arm-wrestle, I'd met Jason Vale under the Throgs Neck Bridge on the Fourth of July sometime around 1990. The place had been packed with people, and when we locked hands, he beat me twice so fast that I was shocked at how easily he did it. We had become friends, and he'd taught me everything he knew about the sport.

Now, at the Rockville Centre, Jason and I were on the table together, and we both did the chalk thing. Jason is a very calm person, not like some of the crazy, screaming competitors I'd met. We locked hands, and chalk fell from them. The ref asked Jason, "Are you ready?," and he said yes. Then he asked me, "Are you ready?," and I said yes. "Ready, go," said the ref.

I hit Jason just as fast and hard as I'd hit all those other people, and his arm didn't even move. Then he let me hit again and still nothing. Then he slowly put me down and won.

When it was over, I had the same smile I always had. I put his hand up in the air to congratulate him. Being a Christian, I know that people are always looking at me to see how I react when I win or lose at arm-wrestling.

People also watched my response to things that happened at work on Rikers Island. For the record, while I worked as a corrections officer, I never cursed at an inmate, disrespected a fellow officer, or did anything that would put my Christianity on trial. If an inmate didn't comply with the rules, it was my job to make sure he did. If I had to use force, I had no problem doing so, for the Bible clearly talks about that in the book of Romans.

Even working as a New York City corrections officer in a crazy place where violence, rage, anger, cursing, and murder are constant issues, it is possible to live the Christian life. I am living proof of this. I have fought the fight and kept the faith glory be to God and you can too.

Yes, there were times when I was scared for my life. One day I was surrounded by thirty-three inmates. One of them was going to jump me, and then all the others would have jumped in. My partner saw what was happening and called for backup. As I waited for help to arrive, I moved backward toward the door. Then suddenly my fellow officers came running in with their riot gear on, and all the inmates ran back to their cells.

CHAPTER 12

Retirement

The time came for me to retire from the New York Department of Corrections after twenty years of service. I'd had an excellent career in the harbor unit and security unit, and I was well liked by my fellow officers.

I had an excellent union president named Norman Seabrook, who always looked out for his fellow officers and their safety on and off the job. He'd fought to get us the best contracts possible and had done an excellent job at it. One of the things I liked most about Norman Seabrook was that he would always say, "God bless." It was a total pleasure to have him as my union president. Even now that I'm retired, he still looks out for us.

Now I'm a free man. I'm able to do everything I'd done before I retired and ten times more. For example, I became a coach for both of my kids' school teams in soccer, basketball, and softball. At night, I'm able to sleep at home with my wife instead of working all different hours around the clock. During the day, I can spend good quality time with my family, go to the gym, work on my magic show, and do a lot of volunteer work with my church and soup kitchens. I do shows for Convoy of Hope, and I like to work with the Lighthouse Mission because, before they hand out the food, they preach God's Word and share about having a personal relationship with Jesus.

I'm able to teach Sunday school and do a lot of evangelism using the gospel magic show. I have also been teaching jiujitsu for free as a means to reach those people who have no desire to go to a church. We train really hard, and I show them everything I know, all while we are listening to cool Christian music. We pray together before and after training, and many times, sooner or later, we discuss salvation.

In all these things, the main goal is to encourage people to live for God in every area of their lives. It is a means of going into all the world and making disciples. Remember that the greatest among you shall be your servant. Always humble yourself before the Lord, and He will lift you up (Matthew 23:11–12).

CHAPTER 13

Thirteen-Year Comeback

Thirteen years after my last competition in arm wrestling, I was contacted by Gene Camp, the president of the New York Arm Wrestling Association, and Jason Vale. They said that newscasters from the United Kingdom who were stationed in New York were looking to interview somebody in law enforcement who knew how to arm-wrestle, and they'd told them about me as someone who not only knew how to arm-wrestle but had a bunch of titles. The news people came to my house for the interview, and it went so well that many magazines in the United Kingdom added it to their press. Their readers ate it up.

Within a few days, Good Morning America contacted me about doing an interview, and they wanted it to be exclusive. I said sure, and they said they could send a limo to pick me up and take me to the city or they could come to my home and do the interview in my gym/garage. I chose to use my house. I called some family and friends to come, as I wanted to get as much of my family on TV as possible. The interview was a lot of fun and was very exciting.

When they asked me about being a magician, I did a really cool "bird" act, and they added it to their video (gma.yahoo.com/video/former-Rikers-prison-guard-gets-132659430.html). I had no idea how big this was going to be. It went viral on national TV across America, but the best part was that they also mentioned that I said we always pray before everything and leave it in God's hands. If you Google my name, you can see all the interviews.

There was another news interview that went all over the United Kingdom, London, and Great Britain. In that video, I talked about how I got started and where I was at, but if you watch closely, you will see where they edited the video to remove what I shared about Jesus. Only Good Morning America kept it in. Check out these sources too:

- http://www.dailymail.co.uk/news/article-2612951/Strong-arm-law-Rikers-Island-correctional-officer-16-INCH-biceps-crowned-champion-arm-wrestler.html
- https://m.facebook.com/revkevjr/posts/10152377388918887?src=email_notif

Another cool thing that arm wrestling has allowed me to do is to share my testimony with youth, young adult groups, and the Convoy of Hope outreach, which reaches thousands of unsaved people for the Lord. I wear my corrections officer uniform and bring my arm wrestling table, which is all cool and attracts more people.

Sometimes I bring a team of helpers. The last time I went, my friend Tommy Wireman came and helped as the ref during the arm wrestling matches after we'd taught some skills. Then he shared whatever God put on his heart. Tommy also helped with the gospel magic shows, and it was a pleasure having him with me. He is also a strong brother in the Lord, which we all need in order to stay strong in God. Remember: iron sharpens iron.

CHAPTER 14

Conclusion

One of the wisest men who ever lived was a king named Solomon, and he said that life was like chasing the wind (Ecclesiastes 1:14). As people, we are always trying to make some kind of name for ourselves in some way or another by being the fastest runner, the biggest bodybuilder, the highest-ranking officer, the richest financial planner, the best arm wrestler, the coolest mom or dad, and so on.

The list goes on and on, and that's okay. We just need to weigh things out. In becoming the best "whatever," did you also become the worst friend or father? Did you put your Christianity on the back burner? All things should be weighed against the most important thing: keeping God at the center of it all.

If you achieve your main goal but do not have God, you have only your achievement. But if you achieve your goal and you have God and your family and friends in the proper order you have it all. You need to know for sure that when your time is up in this world, your sins have been forgiven and you're going to heaven. I once heard someone say that driving a motorcycle at 130 miles per hour on a windy, rainy day in the middle of a storm with no helmet on isn't dangerous compared to not knowing for sure if you're going to heaven.

I truly hope that you've enjoyed this book and that it helps you to become the most you can be for the Lord, no matter what your future holds!

CONTACT THE AUTHOR

magicvinny@optonline.net

(516) 887-1515

Magicbyvinny.com

Thank you, and God bless.